Original title:
Sunset in Paradise

Copyright © 2025 Creative Arts Management OÜ
All rights reserved.

Author: Thomas Sinclair
ISBN HARDBACK: 978-1-80581-520-4
ISBN PAPERBACK: 978-1-80581-047-6
ISBN EBOOK: 978-1-80581-520-4

Twilight's Embrace

The sun slides down like a slick banana,
The clouds are dressed like a funny bandana.
Birds are laughing as they swirl on by,
While the crabs do a jig and the seagulls cry.

Palm trees sway, they're doing their best,
Grooving along in a leafy fest.
Even the sand seems to giggle and spark,
Tickling toes until it gets dark.

A Dance of Dusk and Dreams

As day gives way, the moon trips and stumbles,
Stars poke their heads; oh, how the night fumbles.
Fireflies twinkle like tiny little lights,
And the breeze whispers jokes to thrill in the nights.

The ocean waves laugh, crashing with cheer,
Splashing sailors who hold their drinks near.
Seashells roll by, cracking up in a swirl,
While the sun waves goodbye with a twinkling pearl.

The Golden Hour's Whisper

Gold paints the sky while waves like to giggle,
The horizon winks; it knows how to wiggle.
A beach ball bounces right into a crab,
As laughter erupts, it's a real party fab.

Frolicking fish jump and do a little dance,
While kids on the shore give the sand a chance.
To build castles that tumble with each mighty roar,
And seagulls squawk jokes, always craving more.

Saffron Skies and Silken Waves

Saffron skies giggle as they fade away,
A koala on a surfboard says, 'Come out and play!'
A dolphin leaps, trying to show some flair,
While the turtles cheer, with their laid-back air.

Silken waves shimmer, like laughter in light,
They frolic and spin, happy-go-lucky and bright.
A crab struts by in a dapper bow tie,
Toasting the day with a glance to the sky.

Evening's Serenade

As the day waves goodbye, with a giggle,
The sun does the cha-cha, while shadows wiggle.
Clouds toss confetti, in shades all aglow,
While crabs hold a dance-off, just stealing the show.

Seagulls start crooning, with barely a care,
While friends share a wink, passing nuts through the air.
The waves clap their hands, to the rhythm of joy,
A light-hearted party, just nature's own ploy.

Horizons Kissed by Fire

The sky wears a fire suit, looking quite sleek,
As it struts down the horizon, with a silly cheek.
Butterflies giggle, in a fluttery race,
While the sun plays peek-a-boo, in its golden embrace.

The palm trees are swaying, doing their best,
To moonwalk their way into evening's warm jest.
With a splash of bright laughter, the tide rolls in bold,
As the ocean cracks jokes, surprisingly old.

Celestial Hues of a Distant Shore

Colors splash wildly, like a painter's delight,
The blue crabs are gossiping, all through the night.
Stars begin twinkling, with a wink and a grin,
While the moon takes a selfie; hey, let the fun begin!

A turtle tells tales, of the fish with no name,
In a caper of light, in this twilight fame.
The waves start to chuckle, with each rising beat,
As the sun throws a party, oh what a treat!

Fading Light

The sun takes a bow, with a hat made of gold,
As the seagulls start jesting, being quite bold.
The hues play charades, all painted with flair,
While the horizon waves, with a soft, gentle air.

Palm fronds are clapping, in a rhythm so sweet,
As the shadows grow longer, like a dancer's retreat.
The day bids adieu, in a style quite absurd,
While crickets join in, with the silliest word.

Rising Spirits

Now that daylight's flaked off, like confetti on floors,
The night holds a cocktail, for all of the shores.
Twinkling laughter echoes, in the breeze that's so light,
As the stars mingle freely, in a gala of night.

The moon winks at us, with knowledge and grace,
As we all sip our dreams, in this whimsical space.
So let's dance 'til we tumble, on this canvas so bright,
For laughter's the ticket, to our evening delight.

Beneath the Fading Gold

The sky spills orange juice, it's quite a sight,
A seagull drops fries, oh what a flight!
Palm trees dance silly in a breezy jig,
Toasting with coconuts, feeling quite big.

Sun's slipping down, like a clown's red nose,
Waves are laughing, playing tag with toes.
The beach ball's rolled away, what a tease,
As sandcastles tumble with the greatest of ease.

The Chorus of Twilight

Crickets tune up for a chirpy show,
Fireflies are flickering, stealing the glow.
A fish jumps high, wearing a carefree grin,
Splashing a wave, as if it's a win.

The hammock sways, with a noticeable creak,
As beach towels gossip by the creek.
Flip-flops are lost, oh what a mess,
As they race with the tide in a friendly dress.

Harmonies of the Departing Light

The sun bows low, with a playful wink,
Spilling juice boxes, let's all have a drink!
A crab's on the run, with a burger in hand,
While surfboards are plotting a great beach band.

Starfish are tired, they've danced all day,
Pledging their shells to join in the fray.
The tide pulls away with a giggly cheer,
As flip-flops return like it's their last year.

Twilight's Radiant Secrets

The sky looks like a painter sneezed,
Colors fly out, as if God was pleased.
Clouds wear pajamas, fluffy and bright,
As seagulls conspire, ready for flight.

There's laughter in waves, they tickle the shore,
As barnacles laugh with their crusty rapport.
A dolphin leaps out, but lands with a splash,
Wearing a crown of seaweed, oh what a clash!

Shadows Lengthen

As daylight wanes, shadows grow long,
My cat chases them, thinking they're wrong.
The dog barks loud at the fluttering leaves,
While we sip our drinks, and plot our eves.

A squirrel scampers, thinking it sly,
But grows confused under the pink sky.
The birds start a chorus, but one sings flat,
As we giggle and cheer, shouting, "Look at that!"

Colors Deepen

The sky turns purple, like spilled grape juice,
I wonder if nature's a bit obtuse.
My friends debate over which shade is best,
While I just pretend I'm a robins' nest.

A pineapple slips, and the laughter erupts,
We joke that it's just how dessert interrupts.
The clouds wear orange, like an awkward clown,
And we laugh till we can't, as day wears down.

Whispered Secrets of the Dying Day

The sun winks at us, saying "Goodbye,"
With a flair like a star, in a glittery tie.
We gather our snacks for a twilight feast,
Dancing around like a pancake beast.

A nearby couple tries to catch fireflies,
But they only catch air, much to their surprise.
We chant silly rhymes to the stars overhead,
As night falls softly, like warm buttered bread.

Majestic Fade

The day takes a bow, with a colorful spin,
Laughing at shadows that are racing in.
We burst into giggles, no reason at all,
For the sun's final curtain, we throw a ball.

A rabbit hops in like it's part of the show,
Mistaking the sunset for a disco glow.
We gather our wonders, feeling quite spry,
As the stars appear, grinning from the sky.

Emotions Bloom in Twilight

As colors collide, emotions might swarm,
We dance in the breeze, abandoning norm.
My friend trips on air, and lands in a heap,
We laugh till we weep, till the shadows creep.

The laughing moon listens, a bright giggling face,
While we tell strange secrets, in our special place.
The last light comes down, a ticklish tease,
As we spin in circles, and fall to our knees.

Luminescent Echoes

The sky spills colors like a painter's spree,
Pinky oranges dance, wild and free.
Clouds wear shades, they strut and sway,
As seagulls squawk about their gourmet buffet.

Down by the shore, someone trips on sand,
Laughter erupts, oh isn't life grand?
With flip-flops flying, and snacks in tow,
A beach ball zooms by, like a comedy show.

The Quiet Between Moments

The sun reclines, taking its time,
While crabs in tuxedos perform a mime.
A toddler squeals, ready to dive,
While seagulls ponder if fish can jive.

A sunset snack of popcorn and fries,
As squirrels plot their winning disguise.
Yet, somehow they steal a hot dog, so sly,
The sunset can't stop them, oh me, oh my!

Embraced by a Warm Glow

The golds and purples swirl like a cocktail,
Toasting the day with a fruity exhale.
Bikini-clad folks ride waves with flair,
While a sunburnt dad yells, 'Don't you dare!'

A fire pit crackles, marshmallows roast,
While flops and trips become tales to boast.
In between giggles and silly banter,
The glow keeps pushing, like an eager dancer.

Secrets of the Dimming Light

As the light fades, stars take their cue,
But not before a beach ball takes a run, too.
A surfboard's shadow slips through the sand,
And someone's lost flip-flop takes a stand.

The cool breeze whispers, 'Are you all done?'
But laughter lingers, chasing the sun.
A crab admits he's not a great swimmer,
As night prances in, looking quite primmer.

Day's End

The sky spills orange like a spilled drink,
Birds in a hurry, they never stop to think.
A dog chases shadows, thinking they flee,
While the sun giggles, 'Catch me, just see!'

Flip flops and flip flops, the beach is a race,
Kids with ice cream, all over the place.
Towels are flying, a kite caught in air,
As the day packs up, with room to spare.

Night's Promise

The cookie jar's empty, and dusk starts to creep,
Stars start to twinkle, everyone's asleep.
Moon sneaks a peek, with a grin on its face,
'Don't worry, dear sun, you'll return at your pace.'

The ants are partying, with food that they found,
Little do they know, their dance can't be sound.
In the cool of the night, with laughter and play,
It's time for the sun to just call it a day.

The Melancholy of Departing Light

As the bright ball of fire starts to take a nap,
Clouds fluff their pillows, it's quite the mishap.
The grass whispers secrets, the trees giggle soft,
'Oh dear sun, don't you feel quite aloof?'

Then comes the moon, wearing slippers and glow,
'Don't worry, dear sun, I'll put on a show.'
But the fireball just chuckles, brushes off sand,
'I'll see you tomorrow, you know that I planned.'

Radiant Farewell

Colors parade like a circus in flight,
The sun waves goodbye, but don't you lose sight.
Pine trees applaud, with their needles all spry,
As the sky blushes pink—a delightful goodbye.

But wait! There's a rainbow hiding near warm,
It whispers sweet nothings, all calm like a charm.
Fireflies flicker, saying 'We'll stay up late!'
As the sun tiptoes, it's time to vacate.

Echoes of a Dimming Sun

The day's antics fade, like a scene in a play,
Waves rolling in with a splashy ballet.
Shells dance on the shore, in the twilight hue,
While seagulls reenact their favorite menu.

'Dinner's served hot!' the horizon proclaims,
As shades of laughter swirl, calling out names.
The sun takes a bow, with a sparkle of glee,
While night takes the stage, 'Now it's my turn, whee!'

Celestial Farewell

The sky's a canvas, splashes of pink,
A clown fish wearing shades, what do you think?
The sun trips over clouds, oh what a sight,
Waving goodbye, like it's lost in flight.

Ice cream cones melt, sticky and sweet,
Seagulls play catch, with a fish-shaped treat.
The day giggles softly, as it closes its eyes,
While crabs dance the limbo, under darkening skies.

When the Light Bows

The sun takes a bow, in a sparkly gown,
A horsefly does a jig, while the turtles frown.
The ocean waves cheer, clapping their hands,
As sandcastles topple, like poorly made plans.

The clouds are cotton candy, pink and blue,
While the horizon prepares for its nightly debut.
A parrot cackles, "Look at that show!"
As the stars poke their heads, all in a row.

Evening's Gentle Kiss

A penguin in flip-flops, skipping along,
As shadows stretch out, singing a song.
The sun gives a wink, then it starts to yawn,
While the moon takes the stage like an awkward fawn.

Fireflies join in, flashing their bling,
A raccoon starts dancing, doing his thing.
The light melts away, like butter on bread,
While crickets compose, in a symphonic thread.

Paradise Painted in Shadows

Brushstrokes of laughter paint the warm sky,
While squirrels in tuxedos watch clouds float by.
A pineapple laughs, it's quite the odd fruit,
As night gives a wink, in its sparkling suit.

The waves start to sparkle, with a giggling sound,
As the sun rolls away, not to be found.
Bats in sunglasses swoop down for a dance,
While the world hums softly, in this twilight romance.

Twilight's Serenade

As the sky turns a funky shade,
Birds in shades of orange parade.
A squirrel, shades on, takes a bow,
'Is this fashion? Let me know how!'

Clouds fluff up like cotton candy,
They whisper secrets, oh so dandy.
A rabbit in shades sips on tea,
'Chill vibes, do you copy me?'

The sun winks, a playful tease,
It melts like ice cream with such ease.
The stars chuckle, 'What a riot!'
'Best show in town, you can't deny it!'

With giggles, the light bids adieu,
Night pops up, dressed in dark blue.
The moon shines bright, a smile so wide,
'Guess it's time for the fun to slide!'

Where Day Meets Night

Day says, 'Hey Night, what's your game?'
Night replies, 'Just the same old fame.'
The sun splashes its colors, bright,
'Wanna dance? Let's twirl in light!'

The horizon wears a silly grin,
While clouds plot, 'Let the fun begin!'
A fish jumps up in the sky, so bold,
Saying, 'I'm just following gold!'

The trees sway like they're on a spree,
With leaves that giggle, 'Look at me!'
Day and Night play a silly prank,
With shadows that laugh, 'Let's fill the tank!'

Crisp laughter fills the evening air,
As daywaves give night a friendly stare.
With a final wink, colors collide,
And all join in the cosmic slide!

The Last Brushstroke of Light

Orange giggles as pink sneezes,
Blue paints stars, the whole sky pleases.
A paintbrush from nowhere starts to swirl,
With tipsy hues, it begins to twirl!

Brushmarks dance on the evening glow,
A chubby cloud joins in, feeling slow.
The wind whispers, 'Would you mind?'
Creating chaos, oh so kind!

A dog with a hat pulls up a chair,
'Watching the colors is my affair!'
The sun, like a comedian, tells a joke,
While shadows around him all provoke!

With chuckles, the light takes its leave,
Nights' wild plans, we must believe.
Under the laughs, they fade from sight,
As the world cheers for the stars' delight!

Heaven's Fading Palette

Doodles of colors spill from the sky,
As heaven giggles a soft goodbye.
A cat in a bow tie takes a seat,
'Is this the ending or merely a treat?'

Clouds paint mustaches on the breeze,
As laughter floats through the trees.
A sneaky wind fluffs up my hair,
'Is it fashion week? I do declare!'

The sun waves like a pop star, cool,
As birds in tuxedos make a rule.
With sparkly shoes, they glide and swoop,
Creating a whimsical, joyful troop!

Just as light begins to flee,
The stars shoot out giggles, oh so free.
'Heaven's palette, what a sight!'
Let's laugh together every night!'

A Dance of Colors

The sky wears a robe of glowing hues,
Pink and orange, it's got great views.
A parrot squawks, it's just showing off,
While a crab moonwalks, trying to scoff.

Palm trees sway, with a boogie sway,
As the sun dips low at the end of the day.
Laughter erupts from a distant beach,
Where seagulls gather, just out of reach.

Flip-flops flapping, in a silly race,
Even the sand is losing its grace.
The sun dips low, it's time to play,
In this carnival of colors, hip-hip hooray!

Crabs with sunglasses, just looking so cool,
Dancing around like they're in a pool.
With every hue, the laughter grows,
In the glow of the day, anything goes!

Whispered Promises of Twilight

As the day bids adieu, the giggles ignite,
Twilight's whispers, what a funny sight!
A pineapple winks, it's up to some tricks,
While coconuts chuckle with little quick flicks.

Stars peek out, wearing their best grin,
While a turtle dons shades, ready to spin.
The waves break softly, but loud is the cheer,
With every splash, laughter fills the sphere.

Crickets are tuning their nighttime song,
A crab in a top hat thinks he's the thonged.
As colors merge in a harmonious sway,
Tropical tomfoolery brightens the fray!

Fireflies join the fiesta, alive with glee,
As the moon pulls out its grand Jubilee.
Under stars that twinkle, no one's in line,
In this twilight, everyone's feeling divine!

Glimmers of Serenity

The day tiptoes out, it's quite a display,
With giggles and twirls, come the end of the day.
A shy wave rolls in, wearing a grin,
As the sun waves goodbye, letting fun begin.

Glimmers of laughter, bright in the sky,
A squirrel drops a nut, how could he fly?
Birds in a choir sing silly refrains,
While a starfish competes in the dance of gains.

With ice cream in hand, and toes in the sand,
Smiles are contagious across this grand land.
As the breeze whispers softly, a light-hearted jest,
In this comical paradise, we all feel blessed.

The moon's just a jester, up high in the air,
While the clouds play cards, without a care.
As laughter rings out in the ocean's embrace,
In these glimmers of calm, there's no better place!

Celestial Bliss

The canvas above, painted with glee,
A sunset surprise, come dance with me!
With watermelon colors, oh what a show,
As the ocean giggles, where do the fish go?

Every star comes out, like a burst of cheer,
A jellyfish spins, showing no fear!
Palms wave high, like they're singing a tune,
As crabs shake their legs to the light of the moon.

With sand in our shoes, we laugh and we chime,
The horizon's a sprinter, winning in time.
As the day takes a bow, laughter fills the space,
This celestial joy, an eternal embrace!

Every ripple and flicker, a tickle of mirth,
While the stars play tag, giving joy a rebirth.
In this vibrant glow, nothing's amiss,
Life's a comedy show, in celestial bliss!

Paradise at Dusk

As the sun takes its bow, we all cheer,
Hiding under umbrellas, sipping root beer.
The seagulls squawk like they own the beach,
While kids chase their dreams, but sand's out of reach.

Flip-flops flop as they dance on the shore,
Moms yell for ice cream, craving more and more.
A crab tries to walk with a swagger so fine,
But trips on a shell, and it's comedy time!

The palm trees sway like they're in a show,
Their shadows play tag with the twilight glow.
Bikini-clad dreams with tunes in their heads,
While sand castles tumble, avoiding their beds.

So gather your laughter, let's toast to the night,
With glow-stick necklaces and shorts that are tight.
In this land of giggles and memories we find,
Each moment a treasure, perfectly aligned.

Dreaming in Gold

The sky's painted gold, with a dash of delight,
While fish swim in circles, plotting a flight.
A parrot squawks jokes, and we laugh till we cry,
His punchlines are salty, just like the tide.

Sandcastles lean like they've had too much fun,
Wobbly towers that stare at the sun.
An octopus juggles, what talents he's got,
While beach bums just lounge and tie one more knot.

The waves play a rhythm, a tune made of spray,
Each splash is a giggle, come join in the play!
A turtle sashays, with a hat on his head,
We cheer him along as he weaves through the dread.

With towels like capes, we're heroes at last,
Chasing ice cream trucks, oh, this fun should hold fast!
As daylight retreats with a wink and a nod,
We treasure this laugh, it's a gift from the God.

The Calm Before the Stars

The beach is a canvas, with smudges of fun,
As flip-flops scatter, but we're far from done.
The sand fiddles with toes like it's pulling a prank,
While dolphins dive deep, they're great at their skank.

A lifeguard is napping; he's missing the show,
The kids are now tossing each other in tow.
A beach ball goes soaring straight over the pier,
And a seagull squawks 'mine!' with a frantic veneer.

As ice cream now drips down the side of our hands,
We make silly faces, just like we planned.
A crab waves goodbye, he's the fittest of all,
While we laugh till it hurts, then we take a slow fall.

With laughter as treasure, we count all our days,
In this kingdom of sunshine, we're lost in the maze.
As stars start to spark, let's toast with our dreams,
To the calm before night, where reality beams!

Hues of Tranquility

The colors blend softly, like a painter with flair,
But the dog on the beach thinks he owns the air.
Chasing his tail, oh what a sight,
As sand flies around, what a hilarious plight!

Children laugh loudly, their joy in full swing,
While beach balls go bouncing, oh what a fling!
A seal pops his head, says, 'What's all the fuss?'
And dives back down quick, like it's all just a bust.

Tiki torches flicker, like they're telling a tale,
While someone burns burgers, invoking a wail.
Even the sunset seems to laugh as it glows,
With hues of tranquility mixed in with our woes.

The day wraps up nicely, with beach blankets spread,
We share all our stories, so many misled.
With laughter and memories, we sit side by side,
In this wacky wonder, our hearts open wide.

The Lullaby of Dusk

As the sky turns a shade of lip gloss,
And birds wear pajamas to flip and toss.
The sun waves goodbye with a goofy grin,
While shadows dance around like they're all in.

A squirrel rustles leaves, quite the loud guest,
He thinks he's the DJ, at nature's best fest.
Fireflies blink like they're starting a trend,
While crickets are chirping, 'The fun won't end!'

The clouds serve cotton candy, sweet on the tongue,
While the day's final credits are playfully sung.
With laughter on breezes, it seems they'll stay,
Till the stars join the party at the end of the day.

So here's to the dusk, with a wink and a cheer,
A fun-filled farewell, let's grab another beer!
The night whispers softly, with jokes on reprise,
In this wacky wild world, underneath twilight skies.

Nature's Farewell Performance

The glow on the horizon, orange and blush,
It's nature's big show, no hint of a rush.
Trees are the audience, clapping their leaves,
While the wind starts to giggle, swaying with ease.

A raccoon takes center stage with a flair,
Wearing a top hat, no worries or care.
He juggles acorns, a trick or two,
While the bunnies are laughing, in their best view.

Clouds fluff up like popcorn in the sky,
As if nature is setting up for a pie.
The sun bows down, takes a comedic bow,
While turtles on rocks ponder, "Should we go now?"

As the colors fade, like a soda gone flat,
The owls flex their wings, "Hey, what's up with that?"
The curtain of night brings the end of the show,
But tomorrow we'll laugh at the fun we won't know.

Pathways of Purples and Pinks

In the sky, colors go wild,
Birds wear goggles, looking styled.
The sun dips down, a flaming hot dog,
Clouds do the cha-cha, having a jog.

Neighbors complain, the hue's too loud,
Children call out, 'Look at that crowd!'
A squirrel in shades hits the ground,
Strutting and dancing, so silly and round.

The trees are gossiping, having a laugh,
While flowers bloom in a jolly half.
Petals start dancing, twirling around,
In this grand show, nature's crowned!

As laughter echoes, the stars sneak in,
A concert of crickets, let the fun begin!
The sky bows out, but not without flair,
With a wink and a nudge, bringing joy everywhere.

The Glow Before the Gloom

Lights shimmer as the day says goodbye,
Waves are giggling, like they're shy.
The sun wears a crown of ray-filled bling,
While birds chirp secrets, who needs a king?

The sand's a stage for crabs to prance,
They tango and whirl, giving a chance.
But watch your step, or else you'll slip,
On this wild beach, it's a wiggly trip!

Palm trees wave, wanting a dance,
They sway and twirl, giving romance.
While seagulls squawk like they're in a band,
Playing their sets, on this funny land.

When the daylight fades and giggles ensue,
The moon joins the party, it's a wacky crew!
So laugh and enjoy, let worries be small,
In this golden hour, it's a hilarious ball!

Tranquil Horizons

Colors collide in a jovial spree,
The sun does a dip, looking so free.
A cat on a roof, plotting its schemes,
While bees buzz around, plotting their dreams.

The grass tickles toes as you lay down low,
Feeling the tickle of happiness grow.
A cloud floats by, with a smile to share,
It's puffed with laughter, floating in air.

Fish in the pond begin to wear hats,
Splashing and joking like jolly old bats.
With every ripple, the giggles expand,
Creating a magic, oh so unplanned.

When colors unite in a funny embrace,
The sky holds its breath, it's a cheerful race.
So as day wraps up with a giggly grin,
Tomorrow will bring more laughs to dive in!

Skies Ablaze

The heavens crack open with colors that clash,
As the sun and moon get ready to mash.
A troupe of ducks wearing little bowties,
Quack meetings held as the daylight flies.

The horizon sparkles with silly delight,
Where shadows play games, avoiding the light.
A wandering goat dons a dapper hat,
Posing for selfies, he's clearly the brat.

Clouds become pillows for naps in the air,
While butterflies giggle without a single care.
On this funny canvas, laughter takes flight,
Painting the world in colors so bright.

With a wink, the evening invites us to sway,
Embracing the silliness at the end of the day.
So gather the joy, let the colors amaze,
In this wacky world, we bask in the blaze!

The Promise of Nightfall

As the sun starts to yawn, it spills on the sea,
Fishes are giggling, oh, what could that be?
Crabs in the sand are doing their dance,
While the gulls take a break from the normal expanse.

With shades of pink cake and frosting so bright,
Even the tacos are dressed up for the night.
The breeze takes a giggle, rustling the trees,
Making leaves laugh in the soft evening breeze.

A Tapestry of Dusk

The clouds wear pajamas, all fluffy and blue,
While fireflies gather for a light-up rendezvous.
Oceans throw parties with waves full of cheer,
And the rocks are quite cozy, just lounging near.

As warm hues tickle our sunsetly sight,
Squirrels throw acorns, a comic delight.
The horizon waves goodnight with a wink,
While raccoons gather round for some food and a drink.

The Day's Winding Down

The clock ticks its giggles; it's almost past time,
The sun's wearing shades, looking quite sublime.
Birds take a bow, as they sing out their tune,
And the stars are backstage, ready to swoon.

Breezes start chuckling, the moon joins the fun,
As crickets declare, 'The day's finally done!'
Laughter from children echoes through dusk,
While shadows do pirouettes with a thrust.

Flickers of Joy at Dusk

The sky's a wild canvas, sketched by a clown,
With splashes of orange, pink giggles that drown.
Trees throw their branches, all eager to sway,
While the globe spins a yarn at the end of the day.

Laughter erupts from the picnic basket,
As ants plot their heist with a little bit of brash.
Candles are lit with flames that will dance,
While everyone's toast is prepared by chance.

The Last Breath of Daylight

As the sky turns a silly shade,
I swear I saw a sunbeam fade.
Clouds giggle in hues so bright,
While crickets plot to party all night.

The palm trees sway with a flair,
Screaming, "Who needs a care?"
A dolphin jumps, a wave gives chase,
In this goofy, golden space.

Stars peep out, wearing a grin,
As night prepares to let fun begin.
Fireflies dance with a flash and a twirl,
In this comedic, twilight swirl.

So let's toast to the day's last grin,
With a goofy smirk and a cheeky spin.
Tomorrow's a canvas, so full of play,
In this bright ballet at the end of the day.

Where Heaven Meets the Ocean

Where the sky splashes color, oh what a sight!
Fish are plotting to start a dance fight.
Seagulls squawk with spectacular flair,
While surfers forget they've lost their hair.

The water's a mirror reflecting delight,
As sunbathers giggle, 'Just one more bite!'.
Crabs are doing a comical crawl,
Trying to join seaweed's grand ball.

The breeze whispers secrets, tickles the sand,
While flip-flops take off, quite unplanned.
With a splash and a laugh, the day sails away,
Where heaven and ocean throw a big soiree.

As dusk rolls in with a laugh and a wink,
The sky serves drinks—you know how they think!
To toast to the fun, in this playful show,
Where joy bounces high, like a beach ball's throw.

Coral Clouds and Gentle Breezes

Coral clouds blush, like they stole the scene,
While the wind cracks jokes, barely unseen.
Palm leaves laugh as they wave to the sun,
Saying, "Stick around, we're just having fun!"

The ocean winks, a vast, blue tease,
Wishing for beach gear, a hammock, and cheese.
Seashells giggle, tucked in the sand,
Whispering tales of a whimsical land.

As the day tilts, comedy prevails,
With jokes carried softly on breezy trails.
The horizon chuckles in tones so sweet,
As crabs throw a party on tiny, big feet.

So gather your friends, with sunburns so bright,
Laugh through the shadows, dance with delight.
In this goofy retreat where the sky falls down,
Let's celebrate life in this playful town.

Reflections on a Canvas of Twilight

On twilight's canvas, a mishmash of hues,
The sun takes a bow, without paying dues.
Stars throw confetti, hoping to please,
While shadows giggle, swaying like trees.

A painter's delight, yet absurd we find,
Cows start to moo with a comical grind.
The hilltops smile, wearing cotton candy hats,
As frogs practice croaks that sound like spats.

Fireflies switch on their tiny disco lights,
While owls gear up for their late-night flights.
The moon cracks jokes, with a grin full of beams,
As laughter fills the air, and mischief gleams.

So let's sail into night with smiles galore,
In a world where giggles and gags explore.
Twilight, oh twilight, what a marvelous spree,
In this goofy moment where all can be free.

Colors of a World Unseen

The sky blushes bright, like a cheeky child,
Painting the clouds in hues so wild.
Lemons and limes, purples galore,
Nature's palette spreads, oh what a score!

I saw a bird wearing a tangerine hat,
It chirped at the sun, like, 'Hey, look at that!'
With colors so loud, it danced on a wire,
Making the day feel twice as inspired.

A squirrel in shades, striking a pose,
Chewing on dreams, he's quite the show.
With a wink from the stars, he steals the scene,
Keeping the day fun—and quite the routine!

As laughter erupts from the crickets' refrain,
Life's an amusement, with joy in the grain.
So here's to the laughter as the colors blend,
In this world unseen, where giggles ascend.

Joyful Farewell to the Day

Goodbye to the light, it's time for a giggle,
The sun packs its bags, and starts to wiggle.
With a twirl and a swirl, it gives one last peek,
While the moon, in a tutu, goes 'Oh, 'tis unique!'

A laugh from the stars, as they twinkle and tease,
They're the night's comedians, aiming to please.
The clouds join the fun, turning somersaults,
While fireflies flicker, throwing tiny vaults.

The trees sway and sway, in their evening cheer,
"Who needs the sun? We've got night's cavalier!"
A parade of shadows, the night comes alive,
In the absence of daylight, the jesters thrive!

So here's to the twilight with a dance and a grin,
As the day takes a bow, let the night begin!
Bidding adieu, the sun doesn't pout,
It just hands over the baton, with a shout!

Sunkissed Horizons

Horizons ablaze as the day takes a bow,
It's a race for the ducks, they're quacking 'wow!'
Sunshine drizzles, like honey on toast,
While a puff of a cloud becomes the daily boast.

The ocean giggles, with waves on a spree,
Tickling the sand as it splashes with glee.
Seagulls are swooping, like they own the place,
Hoping to catch a sunset, just in case!

With ice cream cones wobbling in hand,
Children chase giggles, on this golden sand.
A crab in a tux, offers a pointed wave,
Mimicking a gentleman, classy and brave!

So toast to the hours where silliness reigns,
Where golden horizons hold laughter's remains.
With a chuckle and grin, let's savor the day,
For tomorrow will bring more fun on display!

A Raft for Lost Dreams

On a raft made of wishes, we drift and we sway,
With memories bobbing, like clouds in the fray.
Each splash of retreat, a giggle, a cheer,
As dreams come to life, with sound bites we hear.

A dolphin in shades gives a nod and a grin,
Telling us secrets of the fun to begin.
In the water, reflections are full of bright jokes,
Where fish wear tuxedos and giggle as folks.

The breeze tickles feathers, the sun makes us sing,
While clouds share their gossip like a gossipy fling.
Building castles of laughter, we forget our cares,
In this flotilla of joy, nothing compares!

So let's paddle on forward with smiles that are wide,
In a world made of whimsy, on a dream-filled ride.
As the day waves goodbye, we wave back with glee,
On this raft for lost dreams, where we're wild and free!

Melodies of the Dimming Sun

In the sky, colors mix and spin,
Birds wearing shades, let the party begin!
The sun winks, then giggles a bit,
As ocean waves dance, oh what a hit!

Coconuts roll on the light sandy shore,
Crabs join the fray, then cha-cha some more.
Flip-flops abandoned, let's all play,
Till the last light gives way to the gray!

Palm trees sway, filling the air with glee,
Under this ruckus, I spill my sweet tea.
Time slows down, laughter punctuates,
As the lively sky begins to sedate.

With a mango in hand, I'm ready to cheer,
The glow fades softly, my friends draw near.
What a hoot, as shadows stretch and twine,
With goofy grins, we sip sunshine wine!

Softly Dimming Dreams

The sky blushes deep, what a perfect tease,
As frogs start croaking, they sing with ease.
Clouds become pillows, fluffy and bright,
While I chase fireflies, what a silly sight!

Turtles on deck, they wear little hats,
While seagulls play cards, like crafty brats.
Time to wrap up, put the fun on hold,
As night pulls the covers, oh so bold!

Stars popping out, like jokes in a book,
The moon, our coach, gives a wink and a look.
With laughter echoing into the deep,
I tumble into dreams, as the crickets leap.

Those dreams are wild, with racing bears,
And cotton candy clouds, full of sweet affairs.
As giggles linger, I drift on the breeze,
Wrapped in the joy, of night's easy tease!

Embracing the Night's Caress

Fireflies dance as the day shrinks down,
While my dog prances like he owns this town.
Stars yawn and stretch, they're ready to play,
Moon checks his watch; he's fashionably late!

The crickets chirp a ridiculous tune,
While raccoons debate the best way to swoon.
Laughter spills over like soda from cups,
As the evening tickles, and mischief erupts!

Silly shadows cast on the beach, oh my,
It looks like that crab is performing a spy!
We giggle and point as we roll in the sand,
Embracing the night, oh isn't it grand?

But wait, what's that? A coconut tries to flee!
I'm chasing the memories, wild and free.
With the twilight giggles, let's hold on tight,
To this world full of wonders on a mischievous night.

Echoes of a Dying Day

The sun winks out with a cheeky goodbye,
As I trip on a flip-flop and stumble nearby.
Laughter bursts forth in the golden glow,
As shadows leap forward, putting on a show!

The sea splashes back like it's trying to tease,
While my drink tumbles down with the greatest of ease.
Sandy toes giggle, they're feeling quite spry,
As the day takes a bow beneath a bright sky.

In the distance, a parrot tells jokes on repeat,
While the palm trees nod, tapping their feet.
The ocean chuckles, the gulls join the fun,
As I dance with the stars, one by one.

With the breeze blowing softly, as night starts to creep,
I gather my smiles and tuck them in deep.
So here's to the end, a belly full of cheer,
The echoes of laughter will linger in here!

Light's Tender Eulogy

The sun bows low, it's time to rest,
Chasing clouds like lazy pests.
It takes a dip, in a pool of gold,
While seagulls squawk, their tales are told.

The beach chairs snooze in soft embrace,
As flip-flops dance a silly race.
A sunscreen bottle tips and spills,
Reminding me of day's quick thrills.

The ice cream truck plays a jolly tune,
While the sky starts wearing a rosy plume.
Ocean waves wave goodbye too,
In this silly, shimmering rendezvous.

With every beam that bids adieu,
There's laughter shared, so pure and true.
As stars appear, they wink with jest,
For now, my heart is truly blessed.

The Calm of Dimming Radiance

The sun's a clown with a fading glow,
Tossing funny shadows below.
A dolphin giggles, waving a fin,
While beach balls parade, ready to win.

The sky's a canvas, splashed with flair,
Even the crabs begin to stare.
A picnic blanket starts to trip,
As ants stage a hilarious skit.

The palm trees sway with stylish glee,
While sandcastles drink their iced tea.
As glowing lighters spark the night,
The fireflies join the comedic fight.

With marshmallows popping like silly dreams,
We giggle louder, bursting at the seams.
As the world slows down and takes a seat,
The calm brings laughter, isn't it sweet?

When Day Merges with Night

The sun's clock ticks; it's time to blend,
Day and night, they play pretend.
Laughter spills from the fading light,
As shadows sneak, oh what a sight!

The stars giggle, peeking to see,
As the moon rolls in, sipping her tea.
A raccoon struts in a top hat neat,
While sunsets joke, "Let's make it sweet!"

With every chirp, the crickets hum,
A comedy show, oh, here they come!
The fire pits bubble with chuckles and cheer,
As twilight nudges, saying "Draw near!"

The world's a stage, with everyone cast,
As day and night share a laugh, unsurpassed.
With twinkling sparkles in the air,
They dance together without a care.

The Palette of Evening Skies

Brush strokes of orange, pink and blue,
The clouds wear gowns, oh what a view!
Seagulls mimic a feathered show,
While sunbeams giggle, putting on a glow.

The waves recite silly little rhymes,
As kids play tag, forgetting the times.
A ladybug joins on this grand spree,
While butterflies float like they're on tea.

The sand shifts under our playful feet,
As shadows dance a clumsy beat.
A flip-flop flies, but lands in the stew,
And laughter echoes, like morning dew.

The palette of skies, abloom with jest,
Brings joy and whimsy, it's truly the best.
As day's palette fades, this scene we adore,
We'll cherish the giggles and come back for more.

Where Light Meets Lullaby

The sky wears orange pajamas,
As clouds become fluffy bears.
Crickets start their concert,
While seagulls forget their cares.

The sun's got a cheeky grin,
As it slides down the hill.
A toast to the day's wild antics,
With juice that sounds like a thrill.

Stars start to poke their heads,
Like kids peeking 'round a door.
And the moon, full of giggles,
Waves hello with a snore.

Daylight's now a memory,
In this land of twilight play.
Let's dance to these funny shadows,
'Til the night takes us away.

Horizon's Last Dance

The sun wears a big floppy hat,
While the waves do a wacky jig.
Seagulls shuffle their feet about,
As if they've had one too many swig.

Palm trees join in the fun,
Bending like they've lost their mind.
The breeze has a playful tickle,
And leaves come tumbling behind.

Coconuts laugh in delight,
While crabs do their crabby crawl.
As the day takes its last bow,
It's a party for one and all.

So let's join in this whirl,
As colors burst all around.
In the dance of the fading light,
We'll make memories deeply crowned.

Reflections of Pastel Dreams

Brush strokes of pink paint the sky,
As dolphins leap in a waltz.
The sunset giggles softly,
While the waves bring out their faults.

Each cloud's a silly character,
Playing tag with the sun.
As it dips down for a quick snack,
The sea calls out, "This is fun!"

Lemons on the horizon,
Dance like they own the land.
And the ocean's got a punchline,
As it tickles the golden sand.

Let's collect these pastel moments,
And keep them in our hearts.
For tomorrow's another comedy,
As nature plays its parts.

A Symphony in the Sky

The sun strums a gleeful tune,
While clouds harmonize with flair.
In the symphony of the evening,
Even crabs clap without a care.

Colors burst like popcorn,
In a circus up above.
Seagulls sing with all their might,
As fish join in with love.

Stars take the stage like shy performers,
While the moon steps out in style.
Nature's orchestra plays on,
With laughter spread a mile.

So let's grab our imaginary horns,
And join this merry band.
For in this wild concert,
We find joy in every strand.

Embracing the Golden Glow

The sky is painted, orange and red,
While crabs dance sideways, mischief in their head.
Seagulls are squawking, what a loud choir,
As beach balls bounce like they're caught in a fire.

Umbrellas are tipping, drinks spill with a splash,
Flip-flops are flying as folks start to dash.
A kid with a sandcastle, proud as a king,
While waves sneak in just to mess with his thing.

A dog steals a hot dog, running for his life,
Chasing a seagull, avoids an old wife.
Laughs fill the air as shadows grow long,
In this zany theater, we all play along.

With giggles and hiccups, the evening unfolds,
While mermaids whisper, with secrets untold.
So as the sky darkens, we'll keep up the cheer,
In this wacky playground, no room for fear!

A Portfolio of Lasting Impressions

A canvas of colors, wild and absurd,
A painter forgot, so his brush went unheard.
With pinks and purples all over the place,
He's probably regretting that leap into space.

Sunscreen's a fashion, those stripes all askew,
While surfers fall flat, claiming, "I meant to!"
The tide rolls on in, as laughter erupts,
As beachgoers tumble, in waves all corrupt.

Kites are a-flying, but the strings are all lost,
One goes to Brazil; what an unplanned cost!
With flip-flopped adventures, what more could we need?
In a sketchbook of chaos, we've planted the seed.

So let's toast to the moments, the fun and delight,
Creating artworks, 'til we say goodnight.
This gallery's bursting, with giggles and cheer,
In our portfolio, it's perfectly clear!

Softly into the Night

As twilight tiptoes, the stars start to peek,
A dolphin does backflips, while fishermen sneak.
The moon rolls its eyes, says, "Why am I here?"
While lizards are sunbathing without any fear.

Tiki torches wobble, they flicker and sway,
While night owls hoot, thinking it's day.
The hammock looks comfy, with snacks right in sight,
Yet somehow, the dog thinks it's his overnight.

With marshmallows roasting, we tell silly tales,
Of pirates and treasure, and fish with big scales.
But the marshmallows melt, and the chocolate's all gone,
We'll settle for laughter, 'til daylight is drawn.

So softly we drift, into slumber with glee,
The night's full of mischief, wild as can be.
In dreams we will wander, where nothing is right,
And we'll keep on laughing, softly into the night.

Blushing Horizons

The day bids adieu with a giggle and sigh,
While cheeky old clouds race each other up high.
Streaks of bright orange, they scatter about,
While whales play peek-a-boo, oh what a shout!

Palm trees are swaying, like they're in a dance,
Frogs are croaking loud, they look for romance.
With each little wave, laughter bursts free,
As fishes play tag, 'round the roots of a tree.

The sky's wearing blush, it's quite a display,
As bugs try to figure out their dinner buffet.
A crab wears a crown, with a cheeky little grin,
Says, "I rule this beach, now let the fun begin!"

As darkness approaches, a scene to delight,
The stars take their positions, all shiny and bright.
So let's raise a toast to this comical show,
To blushing horizons, and the joy that they sow!

Chasing the Horizon's Glow

Birds in the sky make a mess,
As I try to fix my sundress.
With snacks in hand, I dash around,
Tripping over waves that make no sound.

Seagulls squawk like nature's jest,
Stealing fries, they think they're best.
A flip-flop flies, I chase it down,
Only to find it landed on a clown.

The sun's winking with a golden tune,
While I dance awkwardly, a rubber raccoon.
Friends laugh and snicker, the joke's on me,
But it's all good vibes by the sparkling sea.

As day waves bye with a silly grin,
We sip from coconuts, let the fun begin.
Chasing light till the stars appear,
In this wonderland, there's nothing to fear.

Warmth in the Afterglow

The pie I bake is less than prime,
Turns out my recipe's lost in time.
With laughter echoing in the air,
I blame the oven, it just isn't fair.

Sunrays stretch like lazy cats,
While I juggle drinks and a couple of hats.
Friends point and giggle as I fall with style,
Drenched in lemonade, but hey, it's worth the while.

The warmth wraps us in a cozy haze,
As we share our favorite sunburn phase.
Rubbing lotion on like it's a race,
Losing count of who got the best face.

Chucking sand at my buddy's head,
He retaliates while I laugh instead.
As we toast marshmallows under the glow,
Here's to the fun we all know!

A Symphony of Dusk

The crickets sing their evening tune,
As I try to hold my funky balloon.
It pops too soon, I'm left in surprise,
With a sparkly mess right before my eyes.

Friends giggle and point at my hair,
It's a rainbow explosion; I didn't care.
While the stars twinkle like glittering pals,
We try to count them but end up counting cows.

A squirrel dances, it's got some moves,
While I attempt my own in groovy grooves.
Falling over while clasping a drink,
My friends erupt in laughter; it's a riot, I think.

With the moon peeking, we pull a prank,
Swapping drinks, now that's our rank.
As the day fades, we're all in sync,
Making memories while winking at pink.

Dreams Woven in Rose and Gold

The sky wears colors like a fancy dress,
While I spill my juice all over my guess.
Laughter bubbles up like fizzy soda,
As my snack decides to play the cha-cha moda.

With transitions smoother than my moves,
We laugh 'til our cheeks are in amusing grooves.
A firefly lands on my goofy hat,
And I dance around like a silly acrobat.

As warm light dances across our faces,
We flip through funny old picture traces.
Telling tales of when we were kids,
When ice cream mishaps were forgiven, like bids.

With dreams entwined in giggles and cheer,
We treasure each moment as night draws near.
In this golden hour, with hearts aglow,
We wrap our foolishness in a radiant show.

A Canvas of Warmth

The sky's a painter, with brushes wide,
Swirls of orange while seagulls glide.
A pineapple hat atop my head,
Sipping coconut juice instead of bread.

The beach chairs dance in playful glee,
Each one trying to outshine the sea.
Laughter echoing, a wobbly wave,
Kicking up sand like the best of braves.

Flip-flops flip as I run for a snack,
Tripped on a towel, fell flat on my back.
Yet, with each tumble, giggles arise,
As the sun chuckles in golden disguise.

So here I sit, with grains in my toes,
Wearing a smile, as the cool breeze blows.
A sunset feast of giggles and cheer,
In my happy place, I spread the cheer.

Radiant Reflections

The water sparkles like a disco ball,
Fish doing the cha-cha, what a sight to behold!
With shades that scream, 'I'm cooler than you!',
I strut the shore, feeling fabulous too.

A crab in a tuxedo scuttles by,
He waves hello; I can't help but sigh.
Sipping soda with a twist of lime,
Each bubble pops like laughter in rhyme.

As the light dips down, the jokes ascend,
A hermit crab cracks jokes, he's quite the friend.
Shells in a row, competing for best,
Who would have thought nature loved jest?

With colors that quirk, and laughter so loud,
This beach party sure makes me proud.
So let's raise a toast to the funny and bright,
For every moment here feels just right!

The Evening's Whisper

The sun leans in for a golden kiss,
As evening whispers secrets of bliss.
Sandcastles crumbling like hopes on a run,
But oh, the joy! Who needs to be done?

A cocktail's winking, with cherries afloat,
While seagulls squawk like a comedy show.
Flip-flops misplaced, one under my chair,
I hop on one foot, full of laughter and flair.

The sun waves goodbye, with a sultry grin,
As crabs on parade bring giggles within.
Shadows dancing, embracing the light,
With every misstep, the fun feels so right.

So here we are, in this whimsical land,
With giggles and chuckles, oh isn't it grand?
As night draws near, we'll carry the cheer,
For every sunset is a party, my dear!

Crimson Skies Above

The day waves off with a shimmery splash,
As flamingos strike poses, oh what a clash!
Each cloud a pillow, oh fluffy delight,
With giggles aplenty in this fading light.

Tanned folks sit grinning, some chewing on fries,
While dolphins leap high, hiding their sighs.
Flip-flop races blow up in the air,
Laughter erupts as I run without care.

Evening spreads laughter, a glowing embrace,
With stars peeking in; they create quite the space.
Fires burn bright, marshmallows in tow,
The sweet taste of chocolate gives giggles a flow.

So as the horizon colors all around,
In this silly kingdom, joy can be found.
Crimson kisses the water, steals the scene,
Cheers to the laughter, bright and serene!

The Beauty of Fading Light

The sky wears stripes of orange and pink,
A flamingo lost but too proud to think.
Clouds fluffy like cheese in the dip,
As the sun takes a dive, does it do a flip?

Birds giggle on branches, they cheer,
"Goodbye, sun, we'll miss your warm beer!"
Shadows play tricks, hide and seek,
My toes get chilly; what a sneaky peak!

The trees wear hats made of golden glow,
They dance in the breeze, putting on a show.
The sun waves bye with a wink and a grin,
Leads us to twilight, let the games begin!

So here's to the light that turns into fun,
When day gets tired and night's just begun.
Embrace the chuckles, let laughter ignite,
In the whimsical beauty of fading light.

Crafting Shadows of Night

As evening arrives with a chuckle and chime,
The sun slips away, oh, what a crime!
Moon's feeling shy, makes the stars giggle,
Painting the world with a magical wiggle.

Inky shadows stretch, getting bold in the dark,
Silly rabbits play tag in the park.
The crickets, they chirp, a serenade bright,
While I trip on my feet, oh what a sight!

Fireflies buzz by with a dance and a twirl,
Thinking they're stars, causing quite a swirl.
"Halt!" says the owl, "You can't steal the show!"
Even in darkness, there's laughter to flow.

So tip your hat to the night on its way,
Shadows take over, the silly ballet.
Crafting some magic, as chuckles unite,
In the playful whispers of shadows at night.

The Bidding of the Day

The sun takes a bow, what a quirky way,
Joking with clouds, "See you next play!"
The sky's a canvas, all colors collide,
A true comical circus as daylight subside.

Children laugh loud as the fireflies blink,
Running around, on the edge of the brink.
"Don't catch the light!" a child's warning cry,
But who's to stop when the giggles are nigh?

The trees start to yawn, their branches all sway,
"Time for a nap, we've worked hard today."
While critters emerge, donning shades and hats,
Getting cozy as they gather in chats.

With a wink and a nod, the day says goodbye,
Drawing its curtains, oh me, oh my!
Giggles abound as the stars have their say,
In the whimsical charm of the bidding of the day.

Kissed by Dusk

The sun gives a peck, what a cheeky flirt,
Painting the world in colors that squirt.
The laughter of day hangs in the air,
While night's slyly sneaking with a blink and a glare.

Trees whisper secrets in the soft evening breeze,
As tiny ants scramble, feeling the tease.
"Quick, gather your crumbs!" they giggle and run,
While the sky winks down, nearly done with its fun.

Starlight chuckles, in twinkling delight,
As the moon breaks a grin, "Let's party tonight!"
The whole world joins in, so light on its feet,
As dusk drapes the land, what a humorous treat!

So here's to the joy as day bows away,
With laughter and silliness, come join in the play.
Kissed by the dusk, we all feel its spark,
In the comical dance where day turns to dark.

www.ingramcontent.com/pod-product-compliance
Lightning Source LLC
Chambersburg PA
CBHW072223070526
44585CB00015B/1463